RAF, DOMINION & ALLIED SQUADRONS AT WAR:
STUDY, HISTORY AND STATISTICS

COMPILED BY
PHIL H. LISTEMANN

Drawings by Claveworks Graphic

PREFACE

The purpose of this study is to provide aviation historians and enthusiasts with a range of information relative to each of the Commonwealth squadrons that saw combat during World War II. Each record will comprise a short history, complete with illustrations and artwork, and accompanied by the following appendices:

Appendix I: Squadron Commanders and Flight Commanders
Appendix II: Major awards
Appendix III: Operational diary (number of sorties per month)
Appendix IV: Victory list
Appendix V: Aircraft losses on operations
Appendix VI: Aircraft losses in accidents
Appendix VII: Aircraft Serial numbers matching with individual letters (including mission totals for multi-engine aircraft)
Appendix VIII: Nominal roll (Captains only for bomber and seaplane units)
Appendix IX: Roll of Honour

Individual files will be constantly updated, when any fresh information comes to light. Additional information will be available for download, at no charge, on each squadron's site at:

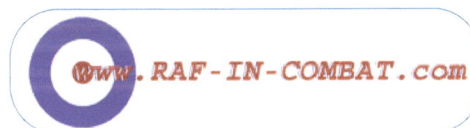

www.RAF-IN-COMBAT.com

GLOSSARY OF TERMS

RANKS

AC: Aircraftman
G/C: Group Captain
W/C: Wing Commander
S/L: Squadron Leader
F/L: Flight Lieutenant
F/O: Flying Officer
P/O: Pilot Officer
W/O: Warrant Officer
F/Sgt: Flight Sergeant
Sgt: Sergeant
Cpl: Corporal
LAC: Leading Aircraftman

DFM: Distinguished Flying Medal
DSO: Distinguished Service Order
Eva.: Evaded
Inj.: Injured
ORB: Operational Record Book
OTU: Operational Training Unit
PAF: Polish Air Force
PoW: Prisoner of War
RAF: Royal Air Force
RAAF: Royal Australian Air Force
RCAF: Royal Canadian Air Force
RNZAF: Royal New Zealand Air Force
SAAF: South African Air Force
Sqn: Squadron
TOC: Taken on charge
†: Killed

OTHER

AAF: Auxiliary Air Force
CO: Commanding Officer
DFC: Distinguished Flying Cross

No. 146 Squadron 1941-1945

ISBN: 978-2-918590-59-0

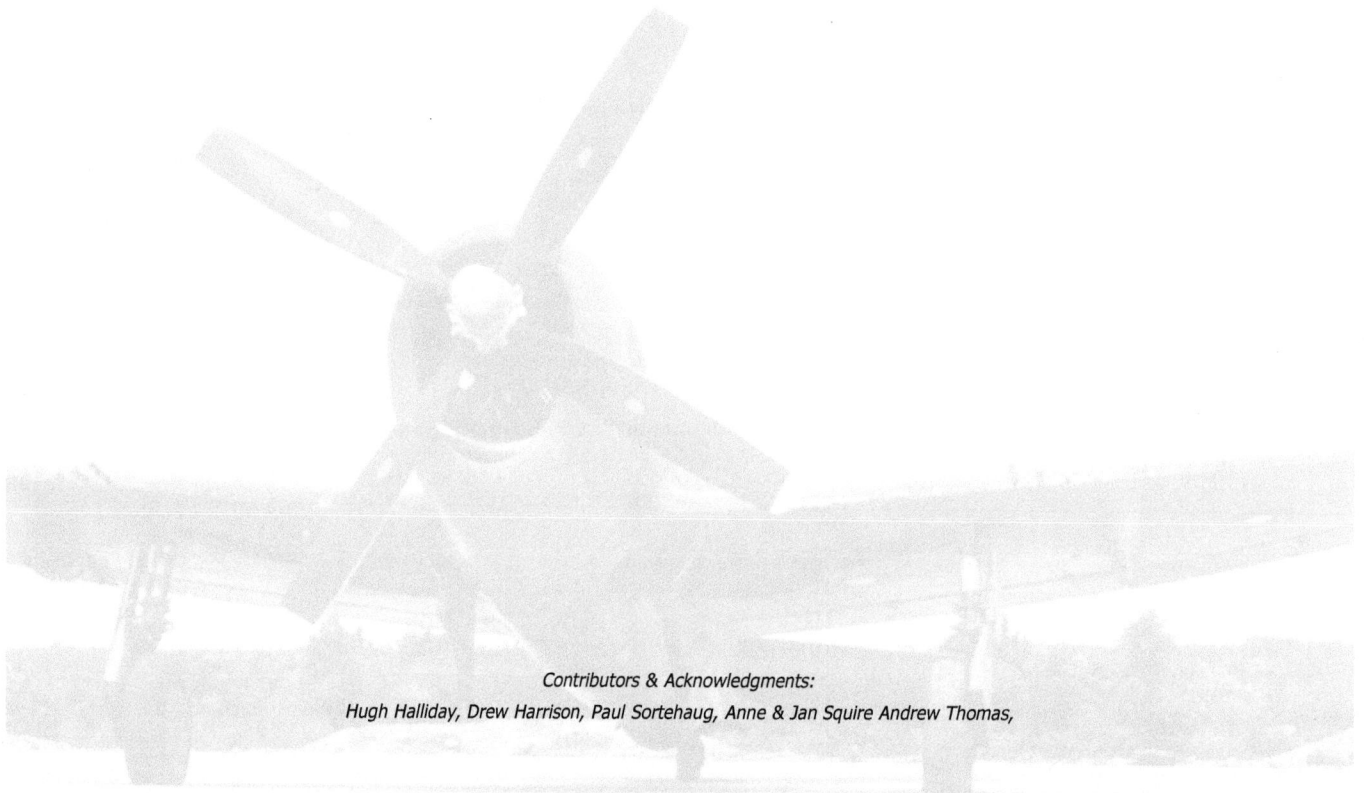

Contributors & Acknowledgments:
Hugh Halliday, Drew Harrison, Paul Sortehaug, Anne & Jan Squire Andrew Thomas,

Cover: Thunderbolt Mk.I FL848 of the squadron waiting his pilot, P/O Edgar Wilson (NZ) for another sortie.

MAIN EQUIPMENT

AUDAX I	**Oct.41 - Sep.42**
MOHAWK IV	**Mar.42 - May.42**
BUFFALO I	**Mar.42 - May.42**
HURRICANE II	**May.42 - May.44**
THUNDERBOLT I	**Jun.44 - Mar.45**
THUNDERBOLT II	**Sep.44 - Jun.45**

SQUADRON CODE LETTERS:

NA

SQUADRON HISTORY

In 1941, with the threat of a war against Japan a probability, the British Empire felt the need to increase the number of it's squadrons in Far East. As a consequence No.146 Squadron was formed on **15 October 1941**, at Risalpur (India), its purpose being to reinforce RAF presence in the North West of India. No.5 Squadron became the nucleus by providing one of its flights, and some totally obsolete Hawker Audaxes. In November the squadron was re-located to Dum Dum, on the north-east fringe of Calcutta, to provide air defence for the city, albeit still with ancient Audaxes. When war with Japan transpired in December, re-equipment became urgent and in March 1942 more modern fighters, Brewster Buffaloes and Curtiss Mohawks, arrived at the squadron. However the few numbers of Mohawk, and lack of spares for the Buffaloes, veterans of the Burma campaign, saw their utilisation only as trainers, before Hawker Hurricanes were taken on charge in numbers from May 1942 onwards.

The squadron became operational on its Hurricanes during summer 1942, and switched to Alipore, also on Calcutta's fringes, in September. From there, it sent detachments to the battle front. However it was not before spring 1943 that it was actively engaged in major operations over Burma, flying Sweeps and *Rhubarbs* against Japanese communications until the end of 1943, and sometimes providing escort to RAF medium bombers. At that time the squadron had a very cosmopolitan mix about it, pilots coming from the whole of the Empire and beyond, something that carried on until the end of the war. On 5th December 1943, during an escort mission, Sgt Dawber claimed a probable victory against a Ki-44, this claim, and a previous single damaged claim, being the only successes reported by the squadron during the entire conflict.

146 Squadron was eventually withdrawn from the Burma front soon after this, and sent to southern India, to counter a rumoured Japanese carrier raid which did not materialise. In June 1944, it began conversion onto Republic Thunderbolts, being one of the two first RAF squadrons to receive the American fighter.

146 Squadron took them into action over Burma in September and participated in that country's liberation, which ended with the fall of Rangoon in May 1945. Sadly, during this period, the squadron lost S/L Hubble on 17 April 1945, becoming the only RAF Thunderbolt unit to loose a CO in action. Operations continued during the following weeks, with the squadron, now fully equipped with Thunderbolt Mk.IIs, carrying out ground attacks against Japanese bases and communications. 146 Squadron's lost its identity on **30 June 1945**, when it became No.42 Squadron, a result of the re-organisation of RAF fighter units in Far East during that summer.

While the squadron did not celebrate the end of the war, in it's original form, it did make a considerable contribution. Despite a lack of aerial kills, more than 3,800 sorties were registered against the Japanese during the last two years of the war. It's ground attack role essentially meant that A-A and ground fire were the predominant danger. It was these that were responsible for the deaths of most of the fourteen pilots who lost their lives, and the two who became prisoners, while serving in No.146 Squadron.

SQUADRON BASES

Risalpur (India)	15.10.41 - 26.11.41	Arkonam (India)	13.08.44 - 05.09.44
Dum Dum (India)	26.11.41 - 02.12.41	Kumbhirgram (India)	05.09.44 - 21.11.44
Dinjan (India)	02.12.41 - 05.05.42	Wangjing (India)	21.11.44 - 18.03.45
Dum Dum (India)	05.05.42 - 06.09.42	Palel (India)	18.03.45 - 23.03.45
Alipore (India)	06.09.42 - 03.05.43	Wangjing (India)	23.03.45 - 20.04.45
Feni (India)	03.05.43 - 26.06.43	Myingyan North (Burma)	20.04.45 - 30.04.45
Comilla (India)	26.06.43 - 03.12.43	Toungoo/Tennant (Burma)	30.04.45 - 06.05.45
Baigachi (India)	03.12.43 - 01.03.44	Myingyan North (Burma)	06.05.45 - 07.06.45
St Thomas Mount (India)	01.03.44 - 05.06.44	Meiktila (Burma)	07.06.45 - 30.06.45
Yelahanka (India)	05.06.44 - 13.08.44		

APPENDIX I
SQUADRON AND FLIGHT COMMANDERS

Rank and Name	SN	Origin	Dates
S/L Bertram **BARTHOLD**	RAF No.33218	RAF	17.10.41 - 31.03.42
S/L Manfred B. **CZERNIN**	RAF No.37148	RAF	31.03.42 - 21.11.42
S/L Geoffrey R.T. **WILLIAMS**	RAF No.41765	RAF	21.11.42 - 09.09.43
F/L Edgar A. **PEVREAL** *(Temp.)*	NZ401029	RNZAF	09.09.43 - 24.10.43
S/L Lawrence M. **O'LEARY**	RAF No.41728	RAF	24.10.43 - 22.10.44
S/L Raymond A.C. **WEIR**	RAF No.119839	RAF	22.10.44 - 09.04.45
S/L Michael W. **HUBBLE** *(†)*	RAF No.49742	RAF	10.04.45 - 17.04.45
S/L William McD. **SOUTER**	RAF No.68755	RAF	27.04.45 - 30.06.45

A FLIGHT

Rank and Name	SN	Origin	Dates
F/L Arthur D. **MITCHELL**	RAF No.33373	RAF	12.12.41 - 02.03.42
F/L Ian L.B. **AITKENS**	RAF No.33777	RAF	02.03.42 - 26.08.42
F/L Michael W. **COOMBES**	RAF No.33561	RAF	26.08.42 - 25.12.42
F/L Edgar A. **PEVREAL**	NZ401029	RNZAF	25.12.42 - 19.11.43
F/L Thomas A. **STEVENS**	RAF No.86669	RAF	21.11.43 - 05.06.44
F/L Raymond A.C. **WEIR**	RAF No.119839	RAF	05.06.44 - 22.10.44
F/L Ray T. **WALKER**	Can./J.11051	(US)/RCAF	29.10.44 - 27.05.45
F/O Ernest A. **FRASER**	BVAF No.1037	(AUS)/BVAF	27.05.45 - 30.06.45

B FLIGHT

Rank and Name	SN	Origin	Dates
F/L Michael **SAVAGE**	RAF No.33370	RAF	14.10.41 - 21.10.41
F/L Charles A. **HARRIS**	RAF No.43400	RAF	21.10.41 - 22.02.42
F/L Helder P.D. **SYKES**	RAF No.77099	RAF	22.02.42 - 24.06.43
F/L Terence B. **MARRA**	NZ403467	RNZAF	24.06.43 - 24.10.44
F/L Herbert A. **IVENS**	Can./J.10649	RCAF	29.10.44 - 11.12.44
F/L Harold A. **BENSON**	Can./J.20350	RCAF	12.12.44 - 20.04.45
P/O Richard **EVANS**	Aus.413481	RAAF	20.04.45 - 30.06.45

APPENDIX II
MAJOR AWARDS

DSO: -

DFC: 4
John Christopher **MUMFORD** (No.156948 - RAF)
Sydney Alfred **PICKARD** (No.188707 - RAF)
Ray Tyler **WALKER** (Can./J.11051 - RCAF), *USA*
Raymond Alexander **WEIR** (No.119839 - RAF)

DFM: -

APPENDIX III
OPERATIONAL DIARY
NUMBER OF SORTIES PER MONTH

Date	Month	Total	Date	Month	Total
Aug.42	44	*44*	Dec.43	9	*1,243*
Sep.42	24	*68*	.../...		
Oct.42	65	*133*	Mar.44	9	*1,252*
Nov.42	4	*137*	Apr.44	7	*1,259*
Dec.42	52	*189*	May.44	2	*1,261*
Jan.43	68	*257*	Sep.44	57	*1,318*
Feb.43	15	*272*	Oct.44	200	*1,518*
Mar.43	48	*320*	Nov.44	281	*1,799*
Avr.43	144	*464*	Dec.44	315	*2,114*
May.43	248	*712*	Jan.45	430	*2,544*
Jun.43	107	*819*	Feb.45	308	*2,852*
Jul.43	67	*886*	Mar.45	387	*3,239*
Aug.43	48	*934*	Apr.45	199	*3,438*
Sep.43	82	*1,016*	May.45	161	*3,599*
Oct.43	108	*1,124*	Jun.45	243	*3,842*
Nov.43	110	*1,234*			
			Grand Total		**3,842**

Extracted from AIR27/989

APPENDIX IV
VICTORY LIST
CONFIRMED (C) AND PROBABLE (P) CLAIMS

Date	Pilot	SN	Origin	Type	Serial	Code	Nb	Cat.

HURRICANE II

Date	Pilot	SN	Origin	Type	Serial	Code	Nb	Cat.
05.12.43	Sgt Neil McK. DAWBER	RAF No.710062	RAF	Ki-43	**HW348**		1.0	P

Total: 1.0
Aircraft damaged: 1.0

	APPENDIX V
	AIRCRAFT LOST ON OPERATIONS

Date	Pilot	S/N	Origin	Serial	Code	Mark	Fate

HURRICANE

02.03.43 W/O Ellis A.G. **COCHRANE**   NZ403950   RNZAF   **BN312**   IIB   †

F/L Pevreal (NZ) and W/O Cochrane took off at 07.36 on a 'Snap recce' for enemy shipping over Akayab. When approaching target at 7,000 ft they were jumped by Japanese Army 01s, one of which fired a short burst at W/O Cochrane. Both Hurricanes took evasive action diving to ground level, where they were then subjected to flak. F/L Pevreal again took successful evasive action, but he lost contact with Cochrane who was believed to have fallen to the flak. F/L Pevreal returned to base at 08.45 alone. Cochrane had come to the squadron in June 1942, having previously served between August 1941 and January 1942, in Europe with No.485 (NZ) Sqn.

Note on the aircraft: TOC No.5 MU 25.12.41, sailed to Bombay, India 03.03.42 in *SS Mocria*. NFD.

02.05.43 F/O John A. **HENDERSON**   RAF No.102617   RAF   **HV418**   IIB   †

F/O Henderson was scrambled at 07.32, leading four other squadron Hurricanes to intercept enemy raid. Flying at 24,000 feet North of Dohazari they sighted 15 Japanese Army 01 fighters, escorting about 10 bombers. The formation was 15 miles away, flying east, with the fighters at 18,000 feet and the bombers 15,000 feet respectively. It was attacked at 08.02 and F/O Henderson failed to return. The other squadron flight airborne soon afterwards, made contact also with F/O A.S. Kronfield (NZ) able to submit a claim one a Ki-43 damaged. However this was little compensation. Henderson had joined the squadron in March 1942.

Note on the aircraft: TOC No.5 MU 09.08.42, sailed to India in *SS Matherang* 08.09.42, arrived Karachi 28.10.42. NFD.

12.05.43 Sgt Frank C. **VERITY**   RAF No.957723   RAF   **HW267**   NA-C   IIB   †

Six aircraft, led by F/L Sykes, took off at 07.56 for a strafing mission over Taungap road. Sgt Frank Verity was hit by enemy ground fire, during the first attack, and his aircraft was seen to strike a hillside whereupon it exploded and was enveloped by flames. He had joined the squadron early in May and was on his second operational sortie.

Note on the aircraft: TOC No.20 MU 30.09.42, sailed to India 30.10.42 in *SS Temeraire*, arrived India 26.12.42. NFD.

30.07.43 Sgt Andrew A. **COWAN**   RAF No.1344898   RAF   **BN221**   IIB   **PoW**

Pilot took off with P/O A.B. Summers (RCAF) at 07.30 to attack targets on the Irrawaddy between Mingu and Chauk. On approaching the target at 300 feet Sgt Cowan was hit by flak. P/O Summers saw him continuing to fly straight and level but then lost sight of Cowan who was not seen again. Summers returned alone at 10.30 and Cowan, who had joined the squadron in May, survived to be taken prisoner being held at Rangoon.

Note on the aircraft: TOC No.20 MU 29.12.41, sailed to Karachi India 02.02.42 in *SS Clan MacBrayne*. NFD.

01.11.43 P/O Francis **FEENEY**   RAF No.129508   RAF   **BH151**   NA-U*   IIB   -

10 Hurricanes led by F/L Pevreal (NZ) took off at 13.25 from Chittagong to Goppe Bazaar, for what was the second escort mission of the day. Their charges consisted of three C-47s of a supply dropping flight. Five minutes after take-off pilot was overcome by fumes, after his engine had failed, and made a crash-landing at Laksham Station. Feeney was extremely lucky and was almost unconscious before grounding and, while the aircraft was totally written-off, he suffered only minor cuts and bruises. Later served with No.123 Sqn, RAF by the end of the war.

Note on the aircraft: TOC No.19 MU 03.01.42, sailed to Karachi India 16.02.42 in *SS Gramanra London*. NFD.

* It is not sure whether the squadron codes letters were used at that time or not.

07.11.43   W/O Edgar N. **WILSON**   NZ411512   RNZAF   **AP916**   IIB   **Inj**

Pilot took off at 20.05, with W/O Harry Aston (RAAF), for a night RHUBARB. Towards the end of the sortie he experienced engine trouble and was obliged to make a forced landing at Ukhia at 23.25. breaking a leg in this crash. 'Neil' Wilson, who had served in the squadron since May 1942, recovered rapidly and was able to complete his tour in November 1944.

Note on the aircraft: TOC No.5 MU 20.08.42, sailed to India in SS Glenifer 22.09.42. NFD.

05.12.43   W/O Francis M. **HORNE**   Can./J.87082   RCAF   **HL802**   NA-J*   IIB   -

Led by F/L Thomas Stevens, nine Hurricanes were scrambled at 10.45 to intercept Japanese aircraft. The squadron was acting as top cover to No.67 Sqn, and made rendezvous at 11.00 over Calcutta at 14,000 feet. Enemy bombers were sighted at 24,000 feet, 35 miles east of Calcutta, with escorting fighters 3,000 feet above them. The formation tried to attack the bombers but the Japanese fighters interfered and a furious melee ensued. F/O Horne's aircraft was hit, and its controls damaged, and the pilot had to make a steep dive from 15,000 feet to escape. Horne was able to regain enough control and make a force landing 3 miles east of Taki, without injury. 'Trader', his nickname, was a Canadian, of Ontario, who had joined the squadron in June 1943. He left the squadron, at the end of his tour, during January 1945.

Note on the aircraft: TOC No.20 MU 20.06.42, sailed to Karachi India 19.07.42 in SS Clan MacBrayne. NFD.

* It is not sure whether the squadron codes letters were used at that time or not.

          F/Sgt Richard **EVANS**   Aus.413481   RAAF   **HV983**   IIB   -

*As above. Evans was chased by two fighters and the engine of his aircraft was eventually hit. He decided to abandon it, and he landed safely by the river, near Taki, suffering just minor bruises. A native of New South Wales, Australia, who had been with the squadron since October, he was commissioned and later led B Flight. He subsequently was to serve in No.42 Sqn for a short time after July 1945 and was awrded the **DFC**. All remaining aircraft returned to base at 12.50 with Sgt Dawber claiming a confirmed victory for the squadron. Both shot down pilots had returned to the squadron by tea-time that same day.*

Note on the aircraft: TOC No.5 MU 18.09.42, sailed to India in SS Strategist 08.11.42, arrived Karachi 28.01.43. NFD.

THUNDERBOLT

02.10.44   F/Sgt Kenneth T. **ORTON**   RAF No.1322067 RAF   **HB996**   I   †

At 12.15, four Thunderbolts led by F/O Benson (RCAF) took off to bomb and strafe Sanmyo. Heavy clouds were encountered at 16,000 feet, as well lightning storms north west of target. The leader decided to abort the mission and the formation headed for base. Around 13.15 the aircraft entered thin cloud at about 15,000 feet and, when they emerged. F/Sgt Orton was missing. It was his first operation and he had been with the squadron for less than two months.

Note on the aircraft: Buit as P-47D-22-RE 42-25928 and arrived in Far East on 30.06.44. Belongs to the initial batch of Thunderbolt Mk.Is received by the squadron.

24.10.44   W/O1 Charlie R. **VERRIER**   Can./R.101326   RCAF   **FL842**   I   †

Led by F/L Harold Benson (RCAF), eight Thunderbolts took off at 15.15 to attack Pantha village. The attack began at 16.10, all bombs falling in the village, which was also strafed, each Thunderbolt making four runs. However light flak located in the north east of the village was reported. During the raid, the aircraft flown by W/O Verrier was hit, while doing a strafing pass, having already dropped his bombs. The wreckage of his aircraft was observed the following day. Four aircraft had earlier that morning attempted to attack this target, but thick cloud between the Imphal Valley and Chidwin, resulted in the pilots, including Verrier, returning to base early. Native of British Columbia, Canada, 'Chuck' Verrier had served overseas since January 1942, and had joined the squadron in October 1943. He was officially commissioned in September 1944 as J.92099.

Note on the aircraft: Buit as P-47D-21-RE 42-25430. Sailed to Karachi in SS Samburgh 12.03.44 and arrived in Far East on 31.05.44. Belongs to the initial batch of Thunderbolt Mk.Is received by the squadron.

11.11.44   W/O Edward R. **GRIFFITHS**   RAF No.1334202 RAF   **FL845**   I   **PoW**

On the day's first sortie, 10 Thunderbolts led by F/L Ray Walker (US), scrambled at 12.40 to attack Meitkila airfield, with Thedaw airfield as secondary target. The target was attacked and the formation turned back at 14.20. Ten minutes later, W/O Griffiths called up to advise that he was experiencing engine trouble, probably caused by small arms fire coming from the ground.

Nothing was heard again from the pilot, who was taken prisoner and held at Rangoon. Griffiths had joined the squadron in October 1943, this being his first operational posting.

Note on the aircraft: Built as P-47D-21-RE 42-25433. Sailed to Madras in *SS Samther* 12.04.44 and arrived in Far East on 30.06.44. Belongs to the initial batch of Thunderbolt Mk.Is received by the squadron.

11.12.44	F/L Herbert A. **Ivens**	Can./J.10649	RCAF	**HD136**	I		**PoW**

Nine aircraft took off at to strafe Meiktila airfiield, F/L Ivens (RCAF) leading. During the attack Ivans' aircraft was hit by flak and crashed onto the target. The remainder of the formation returned to base safely, landing at 16.55. 'Harb' Ivens was captured and sent to a prison camp at Rangoon. A Canadian from Saskatchewan, he had joined the squadron in October to take over B Flight, having previously flown with No.261 Sqn since January 1944. He first served in Canada in Home Defence No.118 (F) Sqn between March 1942 and April 1943, before volunteering for overseas. Liberated when Rangoon fell into British hands in May 1945, he was repatriated in June.

Note on the aircraft: Built as P-47D-22-RE 42-26191. Sailed to Karachi in *SS Homerlea* 15.05.44 and TOC SEAAC 30.06.44. In squadron use since end of October.

17.03.45	F/Sgt Edwin A. **Cattell**	RAF No.700912	RAF	**KJ210**	II		†

Six Thunderbolts, detailed to provide close Army support, took off at 08.30 with the CO as leader. F/Sgt Cattell, No.4 in the first section, experienced engine trouble while still on the runway. As he attempted to taxi off the strip, his aircraft was hit by No.5, Sgt Robert Bourn, crashed and was killed. Cattell had joined the squadron the previous November.

Note on the aircraft: Built as P-47D-28-RE 44-19969. Sailed to Karachi in *SS Sutherland* 30.09.44 and TOC ACSEA 30.11.44. Belongs to the batch of Thunderbolt Mk.IIs received mid-March 1945 when the squadron gave up its Mk.Is for new Mk.IIs.

	Sgt Robert D. **Bourn**	RAF No.1431513	RAF	**KJ367**	II		-

See above. The pilot was injured. The remaining four aircraft continued on with the mission, dropping their bombs. Bourn had joined the squadron in August 1944 and was commissioned (201017). He was with the unit when it was renumbered No.42 Sqn, continuing to serve until the end of the war.

Note on the aircraft: Built as P-47D-30-RE 44-20527. Sailed to Karachi in *SS Fort Jasper* 02.11.44 and TOC ACSEA 25.01.45. Belongs to the batch of Thunderbolt Mk.IIs received mid-March 1945 when the squadron gave up its Mk.Is for new Mk.IIs.

17.04.45	S/L Michael W. **Hubble**	RAF No.49742	RAF	**KL194**	II		†

Twelve Thunderbolts, under the command of S/L Hubble, took off at 15.15 detailed to bomb and strafe Yenggan. During the attack, the CO released his bombs and was pulling out of dive, when for some unknown reason, he rolled to starboard and dived into ground, his aircraft disintegrating in flames. It was Hubble's third sortie since taking over the squadron on the April 10th. The rest of the formation returned to base at 18.15. At the outbreak of war Michael Hubble was with the Territorial rifle brigade, then posted to the Duke of Corwall's Light Infantry (D.C.L.I.) who went straight over to France and was evacuated from Dunkirk. He transferred to the RAF in October 1942 and was soon posted to India afterwards where he became liaison officer with the Army for a long period before he went back to flying with No.146 Sqn.

Note on the aircraft: Built as P-47D-30-RE 44-20654. Sailed to Karachi in *SS Ridgefield* 23.11.44 and arrived Karachi 19.12.44. Belongs to the batch of Thunderbolt Mk.IIs received mid-March 1945 when the squadron gave up its Mk.Is for new Mk.IIs.

24.04.45	W/O Malcolm C. **Keightley**	Aus.416968	RAAF	**KJ321**	II		†

Throughout the day the squadron was ordered to maintain a continuous cab-rank over Oktwin. On the last sortie, while attacking a rice factory, around 16.00, W/O Keightley is thought to have hit a tree, his aircraft being seen to crash and blow up. A native of South Australia, he had served in the squadron since January 1945. Previously, during 1943, he had operated with second line units in the UK. [see also losses by accident 29.03.45.]

Note on the aircraft: Built as P-47D-30-RE 44-20331. Sailed to Karachi in *SS Gera Marquette Li* 23.10.44 and TOC ACSEA 28.12.44. In squadron use since a couple of days only.

25.04.45	W/O Donald D. **Westgarth**	Aus.413463	RAAF	**KJ325**	II		†

The squadron was again engaged in cab-rank operations. Westgarth took off with F/Sgt D. Layland and, on returning to base, he collided with a Harvard of No.261 Sqn (KF109) that was completing a communication flight between its squadron base and

detachments. *The Thunderbolt crashed and exploded on hitting the ground. The pilot of the Harvard, W/O Godwin Scudamore, RAF, was also killed. An Australian from New South Wales, Westgarth had joined the squadron in October 1943.*
Note on the aircraft: Built as P-47D-30-RE 44-20335. Sailed to Karachi in *SS Port Royal* 13.10.44 and TOC ACSEA 28.12.44. Belongs to the batch of Thunderbolt Mk.IIs received mid-March 1945 when the squadron gave up its Mk.Is for new Mk.IIs.

12.05.45   Sgt Allan **WALLIS**   RAF No.1622880   RAF   **KJ237**   II   -
At 15.00 eleven Thunderbolts were called upon to bomb and strafe Letkan. During the outward flight Sgt Wallis' aircraft developed engine trouble and he decided to withdraw from the operation. He returned to Myingyan North airfield, where the aircraft stalled and crashed. The pilot, who was uninjured, had joined the squadron in December 1944.
Note on the aircraft: Built as P-47D-28-RE 44-19996. Sailed to Karachi in *SS British Endurance* 23.09.44 and TOC ACSEA 30.11.44. Belongs to the batch of Thunderbolt Mk.IIs received mid-March 1945 when the squadron gave up its Mk.Is for new Mk.IIs.

31.05.45   F/Sgt Derrick **LAYLAND**   RAF No.1442844   RAF   **KL191**   II   -
At 13.35 six Thunderbolts, with P/O Evans (RAAF) leading, were preparing to take off to bomb and strafe a target at Pyimnakhaung, The aircraft flown by F/Sgt Layland overran Myingyan North, the airstrip, and the undercarriage collapsed. Layland, who escaped injury, had joined the squadron in November 44 and left after another accident the following month [see aircraft lost by accident 29.06.45]. The five other pilots continued the mission and returned safely at 16.05. KL191 was declared Cat.E (total loss) but suprisingly appeared for a couple in Form 541 of 146 ORB in June.
Note on the aircraft: Built as P-47D-30-RE 44-20651. Sailed to Karachi in *SS Ridgefield* 23.11.44. Arrived Karachi 19.12.44, TOC ACSEA 25.01.45. Belongs to the batch of Thunderbolt Mk.IIs received mid-March 1945 when the squadron gave up its Mk.Is for new Mk.IIs.

18.06.45   Sgt Peter W. **HIDGON**   RAF No.1606075   RAF   **KJ293**   II   †
Six Thunderbolts, under P/O Evans (RAAF), took at 07.10 for a bombing and strafing mission near Pyinmana. During the attack Sgt Hidgon's Thunderbolt was seen spinning out of cloud, at 800 feet, and exploded upon hitting the ground. Pilot had been in the squadron less than two months.
Note on the aircraft: Built as P-47D-28-RE 44-20303. Sailed to Karachi in *SS Pere Marquette* 23.10.44. TOC ACSEA 28.12.44. Belonged to the batch of Thunderbolt Mk.IIs received mid-March 1945 when the squadron gave up its Mk.Is for new Mk.IIs.

29.06.45   Sgt Kenneth H. **TREVITT**   RAF No.1607447   RAF   **KJ190**   II   -
Six Thunderbolts took off at 10.45, led by F/O Fraser, for a bombing and strafing mission. At 13.25, having completed their duty, two aircraft collided, while preparing to land. Trivett, who was uninjured, had been with the squadron since April. It is not known whether he operated in 42 Squadron when the squadron was re-numbered.
Note on the aircraft: Built as P-47D-28-RE 44-19826. Sailed to Karachi in *SS Fernbrook* 15.08.44. TOC ACSEA 26.10.44. Belongs to the batch of Thunderbolt Mk.IIs received mid-March 1945 when the squadron gave up its Mk.Is for new Mk.IIs.

               F/Sgt Derrick **LAYLAND**   RAF No.1442844   RAF   **KL265**   II   **Inj.**
See above. Pilot sustained hand injury and probably did not return to operations again. Refer entry 31.05.45 for details on the pilot.
Note on the aircraft: Built as P-47D-30-RE 44-20824. Sailed to Karachi 18.12.44. Arrived Karachi 16.01.45, TOC ACSEA 22.02.45. In squadron use since a couple of days only.

Total: 22

Date	Pilot	S/N	Origin	Serial	Code	Mark	Fate

AUDAX

01.12.41	P/O John **STRATHDEE**	RAF No.111322	RAF	**K3686**		I	†
	Cpl George **CHETLAND**	RAF No.566512	RAF				-

Crashed at Amrotalla Road, Calcutta, cause not known. Stradhee died from injuries two days later while Cpl Chetland survived.
Note on the aircraft:TOC No.10 MU 08.06.39.Issued to No.146 Sqn on an unrecorded date, but it was probably during the ferry flight the accident occurred. No previous use is recorded on its card.

28.04.42	F/L Helder P.D. **SYKES**	RAF No.77099	RAF	**K7356**		I	-
	Sgt Arthur B. **SUMMERS**	Can./R.61466	RCAF				

Took off with 8 other aircraft to practice air-to-ground firing at the Kobo firing range. It was suggested that the aircraft was caught up in the slip-stream of another aircraft and crashed to earth out of control. Sykes had joined the squadron in December 1941, posted from No.5 Sqn. Canadian native of Saskatchewan, 'Ben' Summers was posted overseas in March 1941. Commisioned in January he was posted out in June 1944 and sent in UK where he served with No.1695 Flt with which was killed in flying accident on 09.02.45 while flying Hurricane IIC LF535.
Note on the aircraft: Delivered direct to No.6 FTS 15.09.36. Issued to No.146 Sqn, date unrecorded.

BUFFALO

09.04.42	2/Lt Cecil **ROWE**	SAAF No.102195V	SAAF	**W8246**		I	-

Cecil Rowe was among pilots who were sent to bring back to the squadron some Buffaloes, survivors of the Burma campaign. It was intended they would be used purely as trainers, as all were in very poor conditions. The brakes of Rowe's aircraft failed on landing, resulting in it crashing. The pilot escaped injury and as no spares were available, the machine was not repaired. Rowe, a South African from Transvaal, had joined the squadron the previous month. He was subsequently killed in an accident with the squadron [See entry 08.03.1943 - losses by accident]
Note on the aircraft: Sent from the USA 07.05.41. NFD. Served with No.67 Sqn.

08.05.42	F/L Ian L.B. **AITKENS**	RAF No.33777	RAF	**AN214**		I	-

The squadron was preparing a move to Dum Dum, via Jessore, with two Buffaloes flown by the CO, S/L Czernin, and F/L Aitkens, accompanying it's three Audaxes. Aitkens crashed while making a stop at Jessore, he being slightly injured. Due to lack of spares, the aircraft could not be repaired. Aitkens had been in the squadron for two months, and was to take over A Flight. In August 1942 he was posted to No.17 Sqn. He remained in Far East, and survived the war, becoming CO of No.113 Sqn (September - December 1943) and later No.84 Sqn (September - November 1944).
Note on the aircraft: Sent from the USA 12.06.41. NFD. Served with No.67 Sqn.

HURRICANE

30.06.42	Sgt Thomas C. **GILL**	Aus.402741	RAAF	**BG697**		IIB	-

During the final day of an invasion exercise, seven aircraft took off for the first 'sortie'. All encountered bad weather, and had to make emergency landings, due to shortage of fuel, three in open fields. None of the pilots were injured. 'Tommy' Gill, a native of New South Wales, Australia, was first posted to No.5 Sqn in October 1941 before joining No.146 Sqn the following month. He

subsequently obtained a commission, and remained with the squadron until November 1944.
Note on the aircraft: TOC No.20 MU 18.11.41, sent to FE 06.12.41, arrived in India 18.04.42.NFD.

Sgt William H. **FRY**	Aus.404922	RAAF	**BG716**	IIB	-

See above. An Australian from New South Wales, he had joined the squadron in May. Later commissioned, he was posted during May 1944 to serve No.261 Sqn, with whom he remained until mid-July 1944.
Note on the aircraft: TOC No.19 MU 02.01.42, arrived in India (Bombay) 03.03.42. NFD.

Sgt Lawrence K. **DAY**	Aus.404924	RAAF	**BG969**	IIB	-

See above. Day had joined the squadron in May 1942 with William Fry. In August he was posted to No.79 Sqn RAF, in India, and was killed in a flying accident on 03.12.42 while flying Hurricane IIC BM582. He was a native of Victoria, Australia.
Note on the aircraft: TOC No.10 MU 06.12.41, arrived in India (Bombay) 03.03.42. NFD.

03.10.42	F/O Edgar A. **PEVREAL**	NZ401029	RNZAF	**BN214**	NA-P	IIB	-

During the day the squadron launched a series of internal security patrols (about 12). In the afternoon Pevreal, while diving to disperse a crowd, fired his Plessy pistol, which caused the aircraft to catch fire. He had to make a forced-landing, but escaped injury (it might be also possible that he was shot down by Congress - Ghandi's mob). Pevreal had served the squadron since May 1942, leaving at the completion of his tour in November 1943. A former Buffalo pilot in Singapore, he took part to the defense of the city with No.243 Sqn, then attached to No.488 (NZ) Sqn and 2nd Dutch Buffalo Squadron. Repatriated to Ceylon he joined No.67 Sqn before being posted to No.146 Sqn. In July 1944, he became CO of No.17 Sqn until November.
Note on the aircraft: TOC No.20 MU 17.12.41, arrived in India (Bombay) 03.03.42. NFD.

09.01.43	Sgt R. **CLARKE**	RAF No.1270609	RAF	**BG957**	IIB	**Inj.**

While taking part in a low flying exercise, Sgt Clarke struck a palm tree, damaging his radiator. Following a glycol leak in the cock pit he had to make a force landing, and was admitted to hospital suffering burns in hands and legs. Clarke, who was with the squadron since October, upon recovery did not return to the squadron, and subsequentent fate and postings unknown.
Note on the aircraft: TOC No.20 MU 07.12.41, arrived in India 01.07.42. NFD.

08.03.43	Lt Cecil **ROWE**	SAAF No.102195V	SAAF	**BG812**	IIB	†

Cecil Rowe took off at about 15.05 to a local met recce flight and did not return. Later that day, around 21.00, parts of an unidentified aircraft were found near Barasat. The following day, Investigations concluded that the aircraft had spun in at high speed. Rowe's body was found four days later, but the cause of the accident was never established. [See also entry 09.04.1942 - Accidental losses] .
Note on the aircraft: TOC No.52 MU 12.12.41, sent to ME 12.01.42 later diverted to India and arrived 01.04.42. NFD.

Sgt Stanley H. **WARD**	Can./R.105776	RCAF	**HV820**	IIB	-

See entry 12.05.43 - operational losses for details of this operation. On the return journey the 5 remaining aircraft refuelled at 'Ramu', but Ward had a taxiing accident, the aircraft sinking in soft ground and damaging the airscrew. It was not repaired. A Canadian, believed native of Ontario where he enlisted, Ward went overseas in March 1942 and had joined the squadron in May 1943. By spring 1944, he had been commissioned (as J.88357) and had left the squadron. He returned to Canada in March 1945, being released from RCAF the following May.
Note on the aircraft: TOC No.5 MU 14.08.42, sent to India in *SS Glenifer* 22.09.42. NFD.

31.07.43	F/Sgt David McK. **BLAKCMORE**	NZ411380	RNZAF	**HV430**	IIB	-

F/Sgt Blackmore and Sgt Stevens took off at 11.30 to practice formation flying and collided in mid-air 20 minutes later. Both pilots were able to bale out safely however. It seems that Stevens misjudged the distance, while carrying out a cross-over turn, and struck the leader. Blackmore had been with the squadron since May 1942. He was subsequently commissioned and left the squadron by spring 1944.
Note on the aircraft: TOC No.5 MU 12.07.42, sent to India in *SS Howzones* 08.08.42, arrived Karachi 12.10.42. NFD.

Sgt James C. **Stevens**	Can./R.119486	RCAF	**HW444**	IIB	-

See above. 'Little Steve', as he was known, was a Canadian from Ontario who had joined the squadron in May 1943. Later he was commissioned and left in January 1945.

<u>Note on the aircraft</u>: TOC No.22 MU 14.10.42, sent to FE in *SS City of Cape Town* 15.12.42. Arrived Karachi 31.12.42.

05.06.44 F/L Berry L. **Ulrick**	Aus.413048	RAAF	**LB714**	IIB	-

After returning from a training flight, while in the circuit at Yelahanka, controls jammed and the aircraft dived into ground. An Australian from New South Wales, Berry Ulrick had served in the squadron since October 1943.

<u>Note on the aircraft</u>: TOC No.5 MU 19.06.43. Shipped Bombay (India) 16.08.43. Arrived India 27.09.43. NFD.

THUNDERBOLT

17.07.44 F/L Terence B. **Marra**	NZ403467	RNZAF	**HD101**	I	-

At 12.10, four Thunderbolts took off for a practice formation flight. 15 minutes later, whilst flying through clouds, FL744 flown by F/O A. Kerr (Blue 2) collided with his leader's, flown by F/L Marra. The latter's aircraft sustained aileron damage, and was uncontrollable, and Marra baled out at 1,200 feet. He was knocked out when he struck the ground, and suffered only superficial injuries, recovering quickly. 'Terry' Marra had joined the squadron in May 1942, leaving at the end of his tour in October 1944, his combat service effectively ended. Like Edgar Pevreal, Marra was a former Buffalo pilot with No.243 Sqn in Singapore, with which he claimed one confirmed victory. He was later briefly attached to Nos.258 and 232 Sqns prior the fall of the island, before his attachment to No.488 (NZ) Sqn and 2ⁿᵈ Dutch Buffalo Squadron, in Java. Repatriated to Ceylon, he was posted to No.67 Sqn in April 1942 before joining No.146 Sqn in May.

<u>Note on the aircraft</u>: Built as P-47D-22-RE 42-25933. Sailed to Karachi on *SS Cardinal Griffons* 19.04.44. TOC SEAAC 31.05.44. Belongs to the initial batch of Thunderbolt Mk.Is received by the squadron.

F/O Livingstone A. W. **Kerr**	Can./J.20379	RCAF	**FL744**	I	-

See above. After the collision Kerr's aircraft went into a violent spin, from which he only managed to pull out at 500 feet. He landed safely at St Thomas Mount, Madras, and his aircraft was declared A.C. It is unlikely that it was repaired for it was not issued again to any squadron, and subsequently SOC on 31.05.45. A Canadian, native of Ontario, 'Alley' had joined the squadron in June 1943, and like Marra, was posted out during October 1944.

<u>Note on the aircraft</u>: Built as P-47D-21-RE 42-25432. Sailed to Karachi on *SS Samuda* 14.03.44. TOC ACSEA (No.301 MU) 31.05.44. Belongs to the initial batch of Thunderbolt Mk.Is received by the squadron.

10.08.44 Sgt Geffrey S. **Cumberland**	RAF No.1623541	RAF	**HD111**	I	†

Sgt Cumberland took off at 10.15, as No.2, for a practice formation flight. He made a steep turn to port, which brought him a little below and at an angle to his leader. He attempted to take up the correct position, via a vertical climbing turn, but lost control. His aircraft crashed 4m SW of Yelahanka and caught fire. Cumberland had joined the squadron just a couple of days earlier, it being his first operational posting, and had flown only 12 hours on type.

<u>Note on the aircraft</u>: Built as P-47D-22-RE 42-25943. TOC SEAAC 30.06.44. Belongs to the initial batch of Thunderbolt Mk.Is received by the squadron.

10.11.44 -	-	-	**HB988**	I	-

Caught fire during run up, Kumbhigram, and was totally destroyed.

<u>Note on the aircraft</u>: Built as P-47D-22-RE 42-25920. Sailed to Karachi on *SS Eastgate* 27.04.44. TOC SEAAC 30.06.44. Belongs to the initial batch of Thunderbolt Mk.Is received by the squadron.

29.03.45 W/O Malcolm C. **Keightley**	Aus.416968	RAAF	**KJ308**	II	-

Suffered an engine failure in flight at 09.25, due to lack of oil, and belly-landed in Arakan Yomas near Pauk. The exact nature of the fight is not clearly evident as there are discrepancies between the Accident Card and Forms 540 and 541. The Accident Card states 'Operational patrol', but nothing is reported about this flight on either of the Forms. As no patrols were logged that day, and just one offensive mission was registered, an hour after this loss, it has consequently been recorded as accidental. [see 24.04.45 operational losses for details on the pilot]

Note on the aircraft: Built as P-47D-30-RE 44-20318. Sailed to Karachi in *SS Port Royal* 13.10.44. TOC ACSEA 28.12.45. Belongs to the batch of Thunderbolt Mk.IIs received mid-March 1945 when the squadron gave up its Mk.Is for new Mk.IIs.

05.06.45   F/O Ernest A. **FRASER**   BVAF No.1037   (AUS)/BVAF   **KJ296**   II   -

One of the undercarriage legs collapsed on landing at Myingyan North, after returning from an air test. The aircraft was not repaired. 'Digger' Fraser, a native of Western Australia, had been tin mining in Thailand and Burma. He joined the squadron in October 1942, and was one of the few BVAF trained pilots to have served operationally in the Far East. He subsequently flew in No.42 Sqn when the squadron was renumbered in June 1945.

Note on the aircraft: Built as P-47D-28-RE 44-20306. Sailed to Karachi in *SS Richmond Hill* 30.11.44. TOC ACSEA 25.01.45. In squadron use since April 1945.

Total: 20

APPENDIX VII
Aircraft serial numbers matching with individual letters

NA-A
AP892 *(Hurricane II)*
BS788 *(Mohawk IV)*
HB988 *(Thunderbolt I)*
KJ316 *(Thunderbolt II)*

NA-B

NA-C
HW267 *(Hurricane II)*
FL848 *(Thunderbolt I)*

NA-D
BM927 *(Hurricane II)*
HD118 *(Thunderbolt I)*
KL190 *(Thunderbolt II)*

NA-E
BG961 *(Hurricane II)*

NA-F
HV422 *(Hurricane II)*
FL764, HD127 *(Thunderbolt I)*
HD295, KL315 *(Thunderbolt II)*

NA-G

NA-H
BG946 *(Hurricane II)*

NA-I
HD116 *(Thunderbolt I)*

NA-J
HL802 *(Hurricane II)*
HD117 *(Thunderbolt I)*

NA-K
Z5668 *(Hurricane II)*
KJ181 *(Thunderbolt II)*

NA-L
HV786 *(Hurricane II)*
HD110 *(Thunderbolt I)*

NA-M

NA-N
BG685 *(Hurricane II)*
FL831, HD118 *(Thunderbolt I)*
HD273 *(Thunderbolt II)*

NA-O

NA-P
BN214 *(Hurricane II)*
HD155 *(Thunderbolt I)*
KJ302 *(Thunderbolt II)*

NA-Q

NA-R
HB998 *(Thunderbolt I)*
KL169 *(Thunderbolt II)*

NA-S
FL826 *(Thunderbolt I)*
KL168 *(Thunderbolt II)*

NA-T
HB968 *(Thunderbolt I)*

NA-U
BH151 *(Hurricane II)*

NA-V
FL835 *(Thunderbolt I)*

NA-W
FL748 *(Thunderbolt I)*

NA-X
AP929 *(Hurricane II)*
HD152 *(Thunderbolt I)*
KJ337 *(Thunderbolt II)*

NA-Y
HV983 *(Hurricane II)*

NA-Z
BH230 *(Hurricane II)*
HD128 *(Thunderbolt I)*
KJ224 *(Thunderbolt II)*

NA-?
BE197 *(Hurricane II)*

APPENDIX VIII
LIST OF KNOWN PILOTS POSTED OR ATTACHED TO THE SQUADRON

BVAF

E.A. **FRASER**, BVAF No.1037, *AUSTRALIA*

RAAF

H.L. **ASTON**, Aus.411474
M.S. **BRYANT**, Aus.411838
J.D. **COLLINS**, Aus.403214
L.M. **DAY**, Aus.404924
R. **EVANS**, Aus.413481
D.L. **FRAYNE**, Aus.26774
W.H. **FRY**, Aus.404922
T.C. **GILL**, Aus.402741
M.C. **KEIGHTLEY**, Aus.416968
K.A.C. **LAFFERTY**, Aus.414143
P.V. **MAHER**, Aus.404385
S.D. **MEREDITH**, Aus.406999
G.C. **NORTON**, Aus.400660
S.J. **PRENTICE**, Aus.402135
A.C. **ROBERTS**, Aus.402007
L.R. **SMITH**, Aus.400622
D. **ST-JOHN**, Aus.402939, *NEW ZEALAND*
B.L. **ULRICH**, Aus.413048
D.D. **WESTGARTH**, Aus.413463
K.F. **WRIGHT**, Aus.421651

RAF

R.F. **ADDY**, RAF No.104347
L.B. **AGAZARIAN**, RAF No.133264
G.W. **ALDRIDGE**, RAF No.525653
I.L.B. **AITKENS**, RAF No.33777
S.W. **BALDIE**, RAF No.39481
B. **BARTHOLD**, RAF No.33218
J. **BEATTIE**, RAF No.1569519
J.L. **BEVERIDGE**, RAF No.1550366
P. McC. **BOND**, RAF No.40073
R.D. **BOURN**, RAF No.201017
J.A. **BUSBRIDGE**, RAF No.67055
E.A. **CATTELL**, RAF No.700912
J. **CLIFTON**, RAF No.1795495
M.W. **COOMBES**, RAF No.33561
P.J. **COPE**, RAF No.1217627
A.A. **COWAN**, RAF No.1344996
B. **CROSBY**, RAF No.1321675
G.S. **CUMBERLAND**, RAF No.1623541

M.B. **CZERNIN**, RAF No.37148
N.McK. **DAWBER**, RAF No.710062
F. **FEENEY**, RAF No.129508
S.L. **FORSTER**, RAF No.1107246
C.W. **FRASER**, RAF No.778668
P.O. **GAUGHENBAUGH**, RAF No.1802055, *USA*
R.K.S. **GRANT**, RAF No.1388637
E.A. **GRIFFITHS**, RAF No.1334202
C.A. **HARRIS**, RAF No.43400
D.O. **HAYNES**, RAF No.1165010
J.A. **HENDERSON**, RAF No.102617
D. **HICKEY**, RAF No.153408
P.W. **HIDGON**, RAF No.1605075
W.B. **HOLROYD**, RAF No.101040
R.W.L. **HORSLEY**, RAF No.1386974
M.W. **HUBBLE**, RAF No.49742
G.R. **HULLNECK**, RAF No.776085, *NYASALAND*
J. **HUNTER**, RAF 1342762
J.W. **LARCHET**, RAF No.657281
D. **LAYLAND**, RAF No.1442844
K.W. **LIGHT**, RAF No.171093
N.R. **MADDOCK**, RAF No.1397416
G. **MARSLAND**, RAF No.41940
I. **McLELLAN**, RAF No.1479875
A.D. **MITCHELL**, RAF No.33373
C.G. **MOXON**, RAF No.1377447
J.C. **MUMFORD**, RAF No.156948
J.C. **NEALE**, RAF No.1324749
A.E. **NEWALL**, RAF No.978703
L.M. **O'LEARY**, RAF No.41728
K.T. **ORTON**, RAF No.1322067
S.A. **PICKARD**, RAF No.188707
P.A. **REES**, RAF No.1581960
M. **SAVAGE**, RAF No.33370
B.A. **SHAW**, RAF No.149595
W. McD. **SOUTER**, RAF No.68755
T.A. **STEVENS**, RAF No.86669
J. **STRATHDEE**, RAF No.111322
H.P.D. **SYKES**, RAF No.77099
F. **THOMAS**, RAF No.1803121
N. **TOMALIN**, RAF No.153524
A. **TOOTH**, RAF No.88469
K.H. **TREVITT**, RAF No.1607447
J. **TURTON**, RAF No.124616
F.C. **VERITY**, RAF No.957723
A.G.B. **VERNON**, RAF No.108830

A.M. **WALLACE**, RAF No.1348655
A. **WALLIS**, RAF No.1622880
J.E. **WATSON**, RAF No.1283670
S. **WILLETTS**, RAF No.1583001
G.R.T. **WILLIAMS**, RAF No.41755
R.A.C. **WEIR**, RAF No.119839

RCAF

H.A. **BENSON**, Can./J.20350
A.J. **COOMBS**, Can./J.86592
J.C. **DAVIDSON**, Can./J.15785
G.C. **FROSTAD**, Can./J.10648
J.L. **GIBSON**, Can./J.20381
F.M. **HORNE**, Can./J.87082
H.A. **IVENS**, Can./J.10649
A.L.W. **KERR**, Can./J.20379
J.M. **KNOWLES**, Can./J.20380
J.J. **NOWAK**, Can./J.17255, *USA*
R. **ROSENTHAL**, Can./J.92990
J.C. **STEVENS**, Can./J.91108
R.W. **STRANG**, Can./R.90076
A.B. **SUMMERS**, Can./J.57855
C.R. **VERRIER**, Can./R.101326
R.T. **WALKER**, Can./J.11051, *USA*
S.H. **WARD**, Can./J.88357

RNZAF

D.M. **BLACKMORE**, NZ411380
D.S.B. **BROWN**, NZ414236
E.A.G. **COCHRANE**, NZ403950
J.M. **CRANSTONE**, NZ405520
A.S. **KRONFIELD**, NZ402523, *SOMUA*
R.R.A. **McLAUCHLAN**, NZ404321
T.B. **MARRA**, NZ403467
C.S. **MATTHERS**, NZ403968
E.A. **PEVREAL**, NZ401029
E.T. **SCHMIDT**, NZ414684
M.T. **VANDERPUMP**, NZ40994
E.N. **WILSON**, NZ411512

SAAF

C. **ROWE**, SAAF No.102195V
D.B. **SMITH**, SAAF No.327911V

14

APPENDIX IX
ROLL OF HONOUR
✝

AIRCREW

Name	Service No	Rank	Age	Origin	Date	Serial
CATTELL, Edwin Annesley	RAF No.700912	F/Sgt	20	RAF	17.03.45	KJ210
COCHRANE, Ellis Arthur Gilbert	NZ403950	P/O	23	RNZAF	02.03.43	BN312
CUMBERLAND, Geffrey Stephen	RAF No.1623541	Sgt	21	RAF	10.08.44	HD111
HENDERSON, John Alan	RAF No.102617	F/O	21	RAF	02.05.43	HV418
HIDGON, Peter William	RAF No.1605075	Sgt	20	RAF	16.06.45	KJ293
HUBBLE, Michael Wintworth	RAF No.49742	S/L	27	RAF	17.04.45	KL194
HULLNECK, Gilbert Rodney*	RAF No.776085	Sgt	22	RAF	29.12.41	-
KEIGHTLEY, Malcolm Clair	Aus.416968	W/O	22	RAAF	24.04.45	KJ321
ORTON, Kenneth Thomas	RAF No.1322067	F/Sgt	n/k	RAF	02.10.44	HB996
ROWE, Cecil	SAAF No.102195V	Lt	25	SAAF	08.03.43	BG812
STRATHDEE, John	RAF No.111322	P/O	23	RAF	03.12.41	K3686
VERITY, Frank Clive	RAF No.957723	Sgt	21	RAF	12.05.43	HW267
VERRIER, Charlie Reginald	Can./J.92099	P/O	23	RCAF	24.10.44	FL842
WESTGARTH, Donald Dudley	Aus.413463	P/O	23	RAAF	25.04.45	KJ325

*Born in Nyasaland (now Malawi) from British setlers. Killed in a motor accident.

Total: 14
Australia: 2, Canada: 1, New Zealand: 1, South Africa: 1, United Kingdom: 9

GROUNDCREW

Name	Service No	Rank	Age	Origin	Date	Serial
BARLEY, Colin Noel	RAF No.1270442	Sgt	26	RAF	16.12.42	-
KING, Walter	RAF No.1202544	AC2	n/k	RAF	19.05.42	-
MILNER, Leslie Alfred	RAF No.1429454	LAC	22	RAF	27.01.44	-

Total: 3
United Kingdom: 3

n/k: not known

No.146 Squadron began its existence with ageing Hawker Audaxes (above). Equipped with insufficient numbers of these totally obsolete machines the squadron was little more than a cadre unit. The situation was largely due to the lack of modern equipment, available to the British in the Far East, during 1941. Refurbishment however began during the following year with introduction of such new types as the Bewster Buffalo (middle in No.67 Sqn colours) and the Curtiss Mohawk (below), although No.146 Sqn does not seem to have been put at the head of list of priorities. When the Buffaloes arrived they were survivors of combats over Burma, having seen service with No.67 Sqn, and were in very poor condition. More importantly there were no spare parts, these having been abandoned during the retreat from Burma. Consequently the use of the Buffalo was short and limited. Hope came, for a time, with the arrival of some Mohawks, but the RAF didn't have enough aircraft to fully equip more than a couple of squadrons, and Nos.5 and 155 Sqns were given precedence. The Mohawk was therefore withdrawn very quickly from No.146 Squadron's inventory.
(Author's collection - Audax and Mohawk, Paul Sortehaug - Buffalo)

Following the invasion of the British protectorates in the Far East, the Hawker Hurricane was the only reinforcement available in numbers, the Spitfire not being presented to fighter squadrons until late in 1943. No.146 Sqn was among those units converted to Hurricanes, having worked-up on various other types. Here the squadron's Hurricanes are seen at either Alipore or Dum-Dum, during summer 1942, shortly before the unit became operational. The photo above shows unmarked Hurricanes, after arrival at the squadron (Above -*Terry Marra via Paul Sortehaug, right - Andrew Thomas*).

Above: During summer 1942, No.146 Sqn received more Hurricanes than needed, and consequently BE197 was coded 'NN-?' probably due to the lack of an available letter. However once the squadron became operational, all surplus aircraft, including BE197, were sent back to Maintenance Units. It left the squadron in mid-December 1942. (*Author's collection*).
Below: After a relatively leisurely training period No.146 Sqn effectively began combat operations during August 1942. Up until that time a considerable number of photos were taken for posterity. In 1943 the situation changed somewhat, and photos from that period are not so plentiful.
(*Andrew Thomas*)

The squadron's early training phase was hardly accident free. Right, one of three Hurricanes that had to make an emergency landing, during an air exercise, on 30 June 1942. The serial is not visible but its individual letter was 'N'. No major injuries were suffered by any of the pilots, but all three aircraft were wrecked - see aircraft lost by accident.
(*Author's collection*).
Below, F/O Edgar Pervreal (RNZAF) had the misfortune to make an emergency landing during an internal security patrol on 3 October 1942. He escaped injury although his aircraft was destroyed - see aircraft lost by accident.
(*Andrew Thomas*)

No.146 Squadron was among the first two fighter units to be converted onto Thunderbolts. The replacement of the ageing Hurricanes in their fighter-bomber role had become a priority in 1943, with the offensive to liberate Burma in mind. The Thunderbolt was a second choice for the RAF, after it became evident that there were insufficient numbers of the Mustang, their first preference. Most of these had already been allocated to British squadrons in Europe and the Middle East. Thus the Thunderbolt was ordered in limited numbers, purely as a stop-gap measure, and in 1946 it was withdrawn from RAF inventory. Only 240 Thunderbolt Mk.Is (P-47D-21 and D-22) were built for the RAF, these being replaced by the more potent Mk.IIs, when they became available. At first aircraft were allocated to pilots, like FL848 and HD118, which were flown respectively by F/O Edgan N. Wilson and F/L 'Terry' Marra (both RNZAF). This practice was discontinued by the end of 1944.
(Andrew Thomas)

Squadron's Thunderbolts Mk.Is lined up with the full load of bombs under the wings in October 1944, ready for the next mission. In the forefront HD110/NA-L usually flown by Sydney A. Pickard (RAF). The Thuns have an experimental infidentification scheme showing partial white wings markings painted between the guns and the fuselage while retaining full camouflage on the upper and under surfaces.

No.146 Sqn was allocated a couple of Thunderbolt Mk.IIs while converting onto the type. In order to standardise its flying equipment it reverted back to the Mk.I in October - November 1944. HD295 was one of the few Mk.II models on squadron charge in October that year, and it is seen here with the Thunderbolt identification markings, that had been recently approved. The latter do not conform to the size requirements and they are probably experimental like in the previous page. They were probably painted by groundcrew, in the interim period, awaiting clear instructions. The squadron eventually relinquished its Mk.Is in mid-March 1945.
(*Author's collection*).

By end of 1942 many pilots, in the Far East, were long serving RAF personnel, but with limited war experience, like Squadron Leader Geoffrey R.T. 'Bill' Williams (below). However he was able to count upon the likes of several of his unit, officers like F/L Edgar Pevreal - right - (RNZAF) who had served and fought in Singapore. Pevreal's experience, as it eventuated, proved invaluable during the squadron's first engagement against the Japanese.
(*Edgar Pevreal via Paul Sortehaug*)

Alipore, Calcutta, End 1942/ beggining 1943:
Propellor: 'Paddy' Mahar (RAAF)
Back row - wing: P/O Townsend - believed to be John A. Townsend who was later killed in a Beaufighter in February 1943 while serving with No.27 Sqn -, F/O 'Tommy' Gill (RAAF), F/Sgt Nowak (RCAF-USA), 'Digger' Fraser (Australian - BVAF), P/O Ben Summers (RCAF), F/Sgt J. Collins (RAAF), unknown, P/O St-John (RAAF-New Zealand), unknown.
Front: P/O 'Terry' Marra (NZ), F/O J. Bonner (Adj), F/O Hartley (I.O.), Lt Cecil Rowe (SA), F/O J. Handerson, F/L Tooth, F/O Cranstone (NZ), F/L Helder Sykes, S/L Williams (CO), F/L Edgar Pevreal (NZ), unknown, F/L Blackmore (NZ), P/O J.A. Busbridge, unknown, F/Sgt P. Gaughenbaugh (USA), F/Sgt K. Light, F/Sgt Aston (Aus), A. Kronfeld (Samoa/NZ).

Some of the squadron's personalities:
Left: 'Terry' Marra, another very experienced pilot, who like Pevreal, was an integral cog in the in the squadron's leadership during 1942 - 1943. Below left, Patrick V. 'Paddy' Maher, an Australian from New South Wales. He had completed a tour with No.66 Sqn in Europe in 1942 before reaching the Far East. After his posting to No.146 Sqn he later flew in No.60 Sqn. After repatriation to Australia in January 1945, he started another tour with No.86 Sqn, RAAF in June 1945, and survived the war. (*All, Edgar Pevreal via Paul Sortehaug*)
Below, the young Australian Malcolm Keightley who was killed in action in April 1945 at 22 He had joined the squadron four months previously.
(*Anne & Jan Squire via Drew Harrison*)

Taken at Alipore in February 1943, this picture is showing clearly representative of what the RAF looks like with a mixed a various nationalities. Above: standing, K.W. Light, Douglas StJohn (New Zealander - RAAF), Tom Gill (RAAF), Bill Fry (RAAF) & LLoyd. Front - 'Paddy' Maher (RAAF), Jack Fraser (Australian - BVAF), Joe Nowak (American - RCAF), Max Bryant (RAAF). (*E.A. Pevreal via Paul Sortehaug*)
Below: Rear: D.M. Blackmore (RNZAF), A.S. Kronfeld (Samuan - RNZAF), J.D. Collins (RAAF), Max Bryant (RAAF), P/O E.G.S. Hartley (Intelligence Officer), F/O Tooh (Eng). Front Paul Gaughenbough (USA), W.H. Fry (RAAF) who later served with No.261 Sqn, J.D. Davidson (RCAF), T.C. Gill (RAAF), Joe Nowak (American - RCAF), E.A. Fraser (BVAF - Australian), A.B. Summers (RCAF). Gaughenbaugh and Nowak transferred both to USAAF in May 1943. (*T.B. Marra via Paul Sortehaug*)

Two Australians, photographed during December 1944, upon their return from a mission. Left, Kevin Lafferty of Queensland and right, Ernest A 'Digger' Fraser. Fraser was tin mining in Thailand and Burma before the war, explaining why he was amongst the first enlistees in the recently formed Burma Volunteer Air Force, and also one of the few BVAF engaged in operations during the war. Lafferty had previously flown 33 operational sorties with No.610 Sqn in Europe, between June and October 1943, before volunteering for overseas service. He joined No.146 Sqn in November 1943, leaving in February 1945 at the end of his tour.

SUMMARY OF THE OPERATIONAL ACTIVITY
No.146 Squadron

A/C types	First sortie	Last sortie	Total sorties	Tot Sub-type	Lost Ops	Lost Acc	A/C lost	Claims	Pilot †	PoWs	Evaded
HURRICANE II	08.08.42	16.05.44	1,241	**1,261**	8	10	**19**	1	**4**	**1**	-
THUNDERBOLT I	16.09.44	21.03.45	1,685	**1,685**	4	4	**8**	-	**3**	**2**	-
THUNDERBOLT II	16.09.44	30.06.45	896	**896**	10	2	**12**	-	**5**	-	-
Others											
AUDAX I	-	-	-	-	-	2	**2**	-	**1**	-	-
BUFFALO I	-	-	-	-	-	2	**2**	-	-	-	-
OTHER CAUSES	-	-	-	-	-	-	-	-	**1**	-	-
COMPILATION	08.08.42	30.06.45	-	**3,842**	22	20	42	1.0	- 14	3	-

MAIN AWARDS

DSO: -

DFC: 4

DFM: -

Points of interest :
- One of of the first two squadrons converted onto the Thunderbolt.

Unsolved mystery
Unidentified pilots: Sgt Sullivan (May 42), Sgt John (May 42), P/O Townsend (End 1942) - John Aragon Townsend 115908 ? -

Statistics :
- Lost one aircraft every 173 sorties (155 for Hurricanes - 421 for Thunderbolt Mk.Is - 90 for Thunderbolt Mk.IIs).
- 42.00 % of the combat aircraft losses occurred during non operational flights.

BADGE

A panther's head couped, facing to the sinister.

The badge indicates its activity in Assam and Bengal.

MOTTO

PERCUTIT INSIDIANS PARDUS

THE WATCHFUL PANTHER STRIKES

Authority: King George VI, January 1945

Hawker Hurricane Mk.IIB/Trop., Dum Dum, India, Summer 1942.
Reported at No.20 MU on 13 September 1941, BE197 was shipped to the Middle East on 18 September 1941, arriving on 15 December 41. Following war with Japan, reinforcement aircraft were needed and BE197 was among the Hurricanes sent to India, reaching its destination on 8 May 1942. It was probably issued to No.146 Sqn during summer 1942, but being surplus to squadron requirements it left on 15 December 1942. It was struck off charge in November the following year, seemingly without having had any further allocation. The use of the question mark as squadron marking is unusual, and may reflect the fact that No.146 Sqn had more aircraft than it needed.

Hawker Hurricane Mk.IIB/Trop., Flying Officer Edgar A. Pevreal (RNZAF), Alipore, India, Autumn 1942.
Taken on charge at No.20 MU on 17 December 1941. BN214 was sent to the Far East, arriving in India on 3 March 1942. It is believed that it was among the first Hurricanes issued to No.146 Sqn, although its career with the squadron was short as it was lost during an internal security patrol on 3 October 1942 (see losses by accident and photo p17).

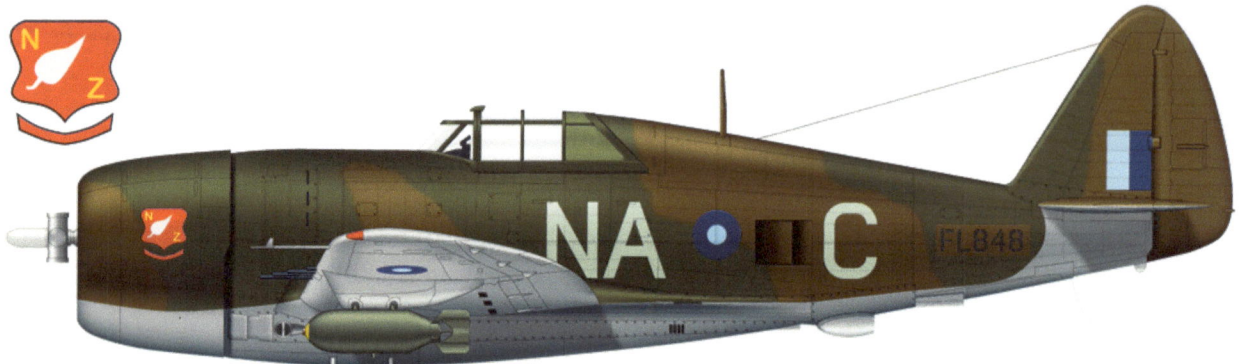

Republic Thunderbolt Mk.I FL848, Flying Officer Edgar N. Wilson (RNZAF), Kumbhirgram, India, September 1944.
Built as P-47D-22-RE 42-25796, FL848 sailed for Karachi, India, on SS *Ocean Valentine* on 6 April 1944, reaching its destination on 31 May 1944. The aircraft was among the first Thunderbolts to be allocated to No.146 Sqn during summer 1944. F/O Ed Wilson (RNZAF) selected this machine as his regular mount and flew the first squadron Thunderbolt operation on 16 September 1944 with it. When Wilson left the squadron at the end of his tour in October, FL848 was flown by various pilots and utilised until No.146 Sqn was updated with Thunderbolt Mk.IIs in mid-March 1945. It is believed that FL848 languished after its withdrawal from the squadron, and was eventually struck off charge in July 1945. The personal insignia is thought to be red and the inscription painted in yellow. After Wilson's departure it is not known if the badge was kept by the squadron.

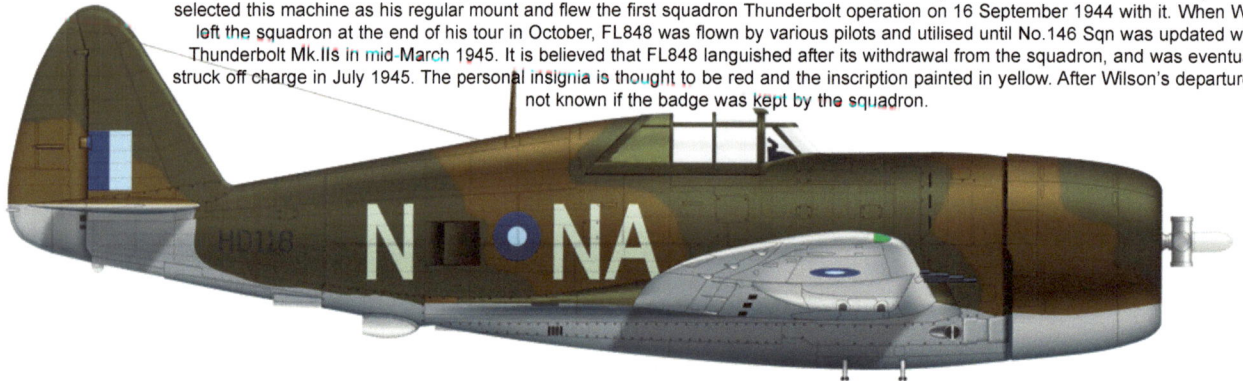

Republic Thunderbolt Mk.I HD118, Kumbhirgram, India, September 1944.
Built as P-47D-22-RE 42-25950, HD118 was loaded aboard of the SS *Frans Hals* on 9 May 1944, reaching Karachi, India, its destination, on the last day of June. The aircraft was issued in September to No.146 Sqn, and was flown by F/L Terry Marra (RNZAF) on 16 September 1944, the first occasion the squadron used Thunderbolts on operations. Another flight followed before the machine left the squadron shortly afterwards, being replaced by HD273 (see below). HD118 resurfaced in mid-December, with a new individual letter, and continued to operate with the squadron until it converted to Mk.II models in March 1945. HD118 later served with No.34 Sqn and survived the war.

Republic Thunderbolt Mk.II HD273, Kumbhirgram, India, September 1944.
Built as P-47D-27-RE 42-26886, HD273 sailed to Karachi, India on 4 July 1944, reaching its destination three weeks later. HD273 was one of the very few Mk.IIs to be taken on charge by No.146 Sqn at the end of September 1944, and was coded NA-N after HD118 (see above) had left the unit. HD273 completed only two operational flights on 18 and 23 October before being passed on to No.261 Sqn after it was decided that No.146 Sqn would continue operations with Thunderbolt Mk.Is. 261 Sqn operated HD273 until the end of December 1944, when a new batch of Mk.II models arrived. The aircraft survived the war although it is not known whether it flew with training units or was simply stored.

Republic Thunderbolt Mk.I FL831, Wanging, India, December 1944.
Built as P-47D-22-RE 42-25779, FL831 sailed to Karachi, India on 17 March 1944 and is thought to have reached its destination in May. Whether it was allocated before December 1944 is uncertain, but No.146 Sqn took charge of it during that month. It served with the unit until the end of February 1945, when Mk.I models were re-allocated in expectation of the arrival of updated Mk.IIs. It is understood that FL831 served with No.135 Sqn, although not utilised on combat operations, and it was SOC by the end April 1945. FL831 features Thunderbolt identification bands introduced in October 1944 to avoid being mistaken for Japanese Ki-44 Tojos.

Republic Thunderbolt Mk.II HD295, Flying Officer Thomas C. Gill (RAAF) Kumbhirgram, India, October 1944.

Built as P-47D-27-RE 42-26708, HD295 sailed to Karachi on SS *Samamola*, India on 22 June 1944, reaching its destination on 31 July. It was one of the very few Mk.IIs to be taken on charge by No.146 Sqn at the end of September 1944, and flew its first sortie on 2 October, Squadron Leader Ray Weir in command. Only two other flights were recorded during the month both by F/O T.C. Gill (RAAF) before the squadron had to relinquish all its Mk.IIs to standardise on Mk.Is. The aircraft is shown with the first provisional identification bands although the size and style did not conform to regulations, which had yet to come through. The propeller hub is also painted in white, a practice widely seen with No.146 Sqn Thunderbolts during the first weeks of use. (see also FL831)

Republic Thunderbolt Mk.II KJ302, Flight Sergeant Robert D. Bourn, Myingyan North, Burma, May 1945.

Built as P-47D-30-RE 44-20312, KJ302 arrived at Karachi on 30 November 1944 six weeks after having left the USA. It is thought to have been stored before being issued as a replacement aircraft to No.146 Sqn at the end of April 1945. It became the regular mount of F/Sgt Bourn in the weeks following, and after the re-numbering of the unit to No.42 Sqn in July 1945. As with many of the D-30 models, the serial was painted in white at the base of the fin.

Republic Thunderbolt Mk.II KL315, Squadron Leader William McD. Souter, Myingyan North, Burma, May 1945.

Built as P-47D-30-RE 44-20904, KL315 was among the first batch of unpainted aircraft sent from the USA. It was stored upon arrival in India in March 1945, awaiting painting in camouflage pattern. However authorization permitting use of non-camouflaged aircraft saw it released on 31 March 1945. KL315 is thought to have been allocated briefly to No.113 Sqn in April, and then towards the end of the month to No.146 Sqn, where it became the mount of the new CO, S/L Souter. Souter used this aircraft during the full term of his leadership, which included the re-numbering of the unit to No.42 Sqn. Following the changeover only the squadron codes were altered, from 'NA' to 'AW'. The latter were painted white on a black panel. KL315 later served with No.34 Sqn before to struck off charge on 28 February 1946. Note that the identification bands were black on NMF aircraft, although on some aircraft these appeared in the same dull blue colour used on the SEAC roundels.

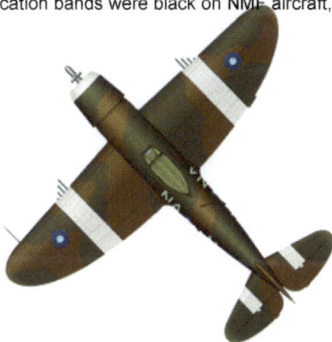

The top view of the Thunderbolt identification bands on camouflaged and NMF aircraft as stipulated by the regulations. The bands were also compulsory on USAAF P-47s.

The Supermarine
SPITFIRE Mk.V
in the Far East

1922-

Vol.
Type Design

Phil H. Listemann

Fighter Leaders
of the RAF, RAAF, RCAF, RNZAF & SAAF in WW2

Volume I

Phil H. Listemann

RAF
at War:
Study, History and Statistics

No.137 Squadron
1941 - 1945

SQUADRONS!
No.2

The Republic
Thunderbolt Mk.I

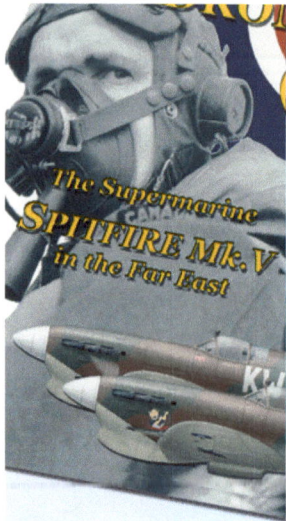

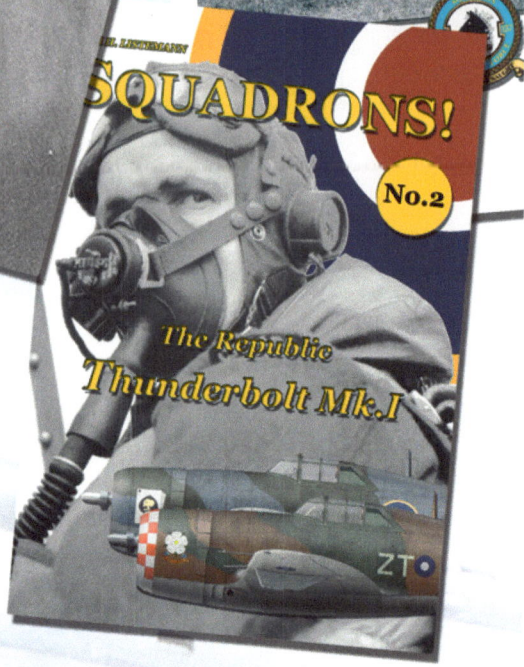

www.RAF-IN-COMBAT.com

- USN Aircraft 1922-1962 -
- Squadrons! -
- RAF, Dominion and Allied squadrons at War -
- Allied Wings -
- Famous squadrons of WW2 -
- Fighter Leaders -

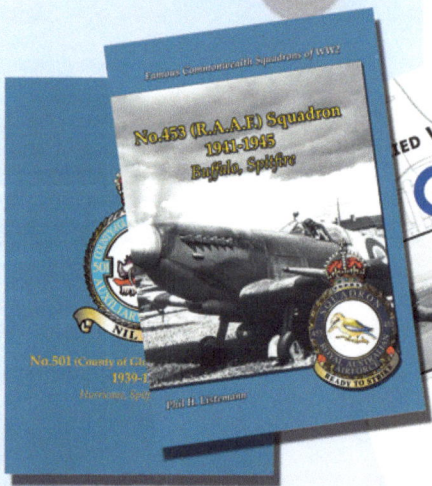

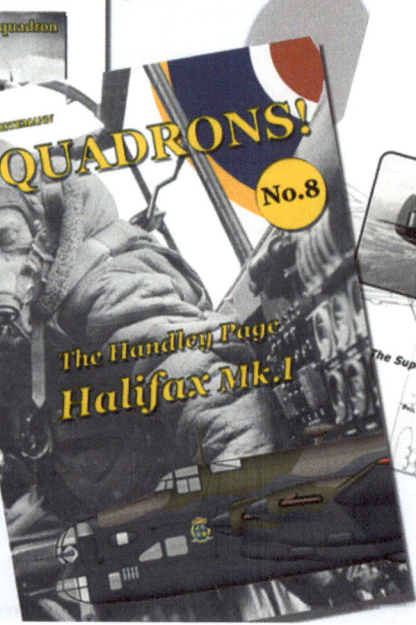

RAF, Dominion & Allied Squadrons
at War:
Study, History and Statistics

Famous Commonwealth Squadrons of WW2
No.453 (R.A.A.F.) Squadron
1941-1945
Buffalo, Spitfire

No.501 (County of Glo...
1939-...
Hurricane, Spit...

Phil H. Listemann

ALLIED WINGS

No.131 (County of Kent) Squadron
...41 - 1945

ALLIED WINGS

Short SINGAPORE III

SQUADRONS!
No.8

The Handley Page
Halifax Mk.I

ALLIED WINGS

No.18
The Supermarine SPITFIRE
F.24